PRAYER
IS FOR
EVERYBODY

Trina McWhorter

I dedicate this book to the memory of my mother, Carolyn Cornelius. She was a beautiful example of love, kindness, and compassion.

FOREWORD

*W*e have been extended the most awesome opportunity to have an audience with God, our Father. Yes, He has invited us to fellowship, to communicate with Him. Prayer is not a burden or an obligation; it is an open door, an incredible opportunity. We neither earned this opportunity nor do we deserve it; we were graciously given it. It is now up to each one of us to take full advantage of it. Prayer brings us into the presence of a loving Father, not a vengeful God, to be blessed by His love, not to be cursed by His anger.

Prayer is not a time to try to impress God or to appear to be something or someone we are not. It is an opportunity to be intimate with the Father, a time to be transparent, vulnerable, and honest. It is a time to give voice to the sentiments, hurts, frustrations, disappointments, and the desires of our hearts. This invitation is not just to a certain class of believers. It is for all of the Father's children: the mature and the immature, the new believer and the older believer, the carnal and the spiritual, the faithful and the unfaithful. Yes, Prayer is 4 all.

In prayer, I show my gratitude to God. I acknowledge the good He has done and the good He is. I acknowledge His greatness, His holiness, His uniqueness, and His sovereignty. It is an opportunity to unload on Him, to release my cares, my burdens, and my worries. It is in prayer that I invite and welcome Him into my life, my problems, and my needs. I acknowledge my limitations and God's limitless ability. Prayer is not just an opportunity to tell the Father what I want. It is also for me to discover what He wants and to choose His will over mine.

It is in prayer that I come against all that has come against me and my purpose. I gain and access victory through prayer. Prayer not only changes my situation, more importantly, it changes me. It changes my attitude, perspective, desires, and expectations. It is an opportunity to move beyond myself and selfishness, so I can pray and intercede on the behalf of others. In intercession, my needs and desires take the back seat to others' needs and their desires. It is a time for me to willingly forgive those who have knowingly and unknowingly wronged me as I embrace and receive the forgiveness my Father willingly offers me.

Prayer is communication. Therefore, it is not just me talking to the Father; it is also me allowing the Father to speak to me. I must give Him an opportunity to talk. I must be still and intentionally listen to what He desires to say.

He has what I need. Then finally, I thank Him for answering me even before my natural eyes see answers.

Trina McWhorter leads the Intercessory Ministry at LIFE Church, the church where I pastor in Atlanta, GA. She and her team lead our congregation in prayer daily. They lead us in a time of corporate prayer prior to each service. They also lead the congregation in a monthly 12-hour prayer and fasting chain. Prayer is her passion. Not only is she passionate about prayer, but she has taught many how to pray, create, and maintain a passionate life of prayer.

In *Prayer is 4 Everybody*, Trina McWhorter will ignite your prayer life and your church's prayer ministry. She will make the case that all are called to pray and will encourage all to embrace and fully exercise this incredible opportunity to commune with the Creator, the Sovereign, our Father. So, don't wait; say something to Him now. He is waiting, longing, to hear from YOU. Go ahead, and say something because "Prayer is 4 you. Prayer is 4 everybody!"

Pastor Terence A. Merritt, M.D.

Table of Contents

FOREWORD ....*iii*

INTRODUCTION ....*viii*

CHAPTER 1 ....*1*

YOUR PRAYERS ARE IMPORTANT............ *1*

CHAPTER 2 ....*9*

PERFECT PEOPLE NOT ALLOWED............ *9*

CHAPTER 3 ....*17*

NO SHADE, ALL LOVE............................. *17*

CHAPTER 4 ....*29*

VALUABLE EXCHANGE *29*

CHAPTER 5 ....*51*

FAITH *51*

MEDITATION SCRIPTURES....................... *59*

INTRODUCTION

I cannot imagine waking up in the morning without having a conversation with my Father. My day is filled interceding for others, as well as impromptu prayer, praise, and worship. Prayer has been my comfort through every high and low in my life. It made the unexplainable things bearable. It has given me peace and comfort when nothing or no one else could. Prayer gradually developed a relationship with the Father I would never have known was possible had I not been introduced to the power daily, consistent communication with Him holds. I now realize that great treasures and mysteries unfold as you sit in the presence of God, soaking up His love, and revealing to Him the deepest, most intimate cries of your heart.

My understanding, enjoyment, and love for prayer and the power that lies in it have not always been as great as they are now. It took time, commitment, and perseverance. The love I have for prayer came because I pressed myself to stay on the journey of seeking God ⏀ whether I saw any change or not.

Over twenty years ago, my then pastor, the late Nathan Simmons told me that prayer would connect me to God in a way that nothing else could or ever would. That's when I started my prayer life. His statement peaked my curiosity and whet an appetite I never knew existed deep inside. Little did I know a seed had been planted in me that would take my life to heights and depths I never imagined possible.

At the beginning of my prayer life, I would talk to God not knowing exactly what I was doing or how it worked. I felt awkward. I even tried copying the more experienced believers (seasoned saints). I imitated what they were doing. However, it seemed fake and just plain wrong. As I sat and listened to what was being said, I got a revelation. I realized that as I focused on God and simply said "Thank You," I would feel His presence.

This was getting interesting.

At times, in worship, the words would just flow effortlessly. And so, as I moved with determination and ignored my feelings, the authenticity and second-nature flow of prayer were being birthed in me. I must admit there were times when doubt and discouragement reared their ugly heads. I would focus on the thoughts that came to my mind: "Are you talking to yourself?" "Does God hear you?" These thoughts were confusing. Nevertheless, God always used something or someone to push me back in alignment with His plans to meet me in prayer.

I took strength from the scripture that told me if I seek, I would find (Matthew 7:7). The Enemy was relentless in attacking me. I would hear him say, "You aren't good enough to talk to God" or "You're bothering Him with your petty requests." But I would open God's Word and find what I needed to keep moving on my quest to know God. God's Word would mute the suggestions of the Enemy and allow me to focus on the new creature God said I was and the promises He said belonged to me. These experiences taught me that God doesn't hear us based on seniority. Rather, He hears the words of His newest to His most mature sons and daughters.

I began to see that God is not biased. To Him, there is no difference between someone like me, who didn't grow up in the church and who had made many mistakes and those who were born and raised in the church. This revelation was soothing, yet, perplexing to me. I was comforted by the fact that God loved unconditionally, but I was perplexed because I didn't know why. I wasn't as polished as others who understood what it meant to have a relationship with God through prayer. Yet, He chooses to let me feel His presence when I set aside time to pray.

The Word built my spiritual muscle (faith) so I could continue on the road to having a relationship with God. I gained strength and courage to commune with this God who told me He wanted me regardless of my past or my present.

The Word created a longing to pray like other men and women I heard call God's name and His presence would just show up. I was eager and inspired. I wanted to know how to get so caught up in prayer and worship that people would be healed and blessed. As I listened and watched others pray I knew they were in a different dimension with God.

I believe this was similar to David's experience in the Psalm:

As the deer panteth after the water brook so panteth my soul after thee, O God. My soul thirsteth for God, for the living God: When shall I come to appear before thee?

(Psalm 42:1-2).

The hunger I felt produced more confidence in me and dared me to believe that God heard me every time I prayed. I started to hear the Holy Spirit speak to me as I set aside time to show God my relationship with Him was the most important one I had ever entered. What I experienced next was totally unexpected. I felt the presence of God before I initiated contact. I started feeling the presence of God in places other than church and in my worship time. It was definitely becoming a relationship and just like in natural relationships when both parties are all in, the perception of what should be expected from that relationship changes.

Perception

This is to become aware of something by use of the senses; especially through sight (Oxford Dictionary.com)

I Was Blind, but Now, I see.

When I began to see, understand, and accept that God was pleased to meet me on our prayer dates, my view of Him changed. I slowly started to see the scary picture of God that had been painted by well-meaning Christians was wrong. He did not want me or any believer to see Him that way. I realized He wasn't holding any grudges against those He proclaimed He loves.

Figuring this out was a process. You see, many of the sermons of that time were steeped with admonitions of "Woe be unto you" or "Be careful of the wrath of God." Few spoke about the love and grace of God. I can't say I didn't clam up a few times with the feeling God didn't like me but thank God it didn't last. I would pray and ask God for stuff, pray for others or just say "I love You" or "Thank You." Searching the scriptures became my favorite past time. I was seeking answers and evidence of God's unconditional love and desire for me. My search started a renovation in my mind that changed how I lived and the decisions I made. I was being transformed into a new creature just like the Bible said.

Shake, Rattle, and Roll

I started to see from God's perspective and consequently, I felt things erupting on the inside. The things I thought were worth my time began to change. What I thought was important changed drastically as I let the Holy Spirit lead me. My palate became more discriminating. I couldn't talk the same way, listen to the same things or even watch pictures I thought would pollute my mind. I lost my appetite for those things, but I craved anything that would educate me on prayer.

Through studying, I found a new passion. It outweighed my zeal for people, things, my career, and family. I was so passionate, I no longer needed to wait for the worship leader to tell me lift my hands in thanksgiving. There was a built-in gratitude that wouldn't let me be quiet. As I reflect on this small excerpt on maturing in prayer, I realize I am still growing. I am grateful I am still hungry for more of God. Just as I couldn't be quiet then, I can't be quiet now. I am so enthusiastic about prayer that I am eager for other believers to connect with God beyond the routine of a surface relationship.

If you start or reignite a prayer relationship

with God, you will go beyond what you've previously experienced in your life or watched others experience. There is no pinnacle of our prayer conversations with God and the answers and manifestation that come from those conversations. God will allow you to go as high as you are willing to go. He will feed those who are hungry for Him and what He loves, no matter how ferocious that appetite may become. People who are willing to challenge and discipline themselves by pressing into God's presence will see what is not seen by the natural eye.

Many of us get stuck at the stage of courtship with God. As in our human love relationships, courtship is never meant to be permanent. Rather, it is intended to move us into a deeper more binding commitment. It carries us to the point of the relationship where we are given rights that are not present in courtship. Remaining in a permanent courtship is like settling for an appetizer when God has a full-course meal prepared for each of us. Courtship will never suffice when you allow pure passion to be developed, Surface admiration won't move you because you've become used to intimacy that can't be satisfied by anything less.

I invite you to take your personal journey to find out how much God is in love with you. He loves you regardless of how you have lived or are currently living your life. Are you looking for something different in your new relationship with God? Do you want to put the fire back into your relationship with Him? Prayer is the answer. It will make the difference. The distinction between friendship with God and intimacy with Him is the way we see Him and how we believe He sees us. Knowing you are loved without reservation creates a deeper intimacy. Moreover, the manifestation of such love is bigger in your life and in everything you set out to do.

Understanding the love of God and receiving it opens up His promises in a more spectacular way. You feel more secure knowing you don't have to be perfect to receive God's promises; every one of them belongs to you. I offer you a thought that will change your spiritual, as well as your natural life - Prayer is 4 you. *Prayer is 4 everybody*.

CHAPTER 1

YOUR PRAYERS ARE IMPORTANT

I pray that by the time you are finished reading this book an intense hunger for prayer will be stirred in you. As a result of that stirring, your life will be enriched in unimaginable ways. I want to eradicate the thought from your mind that prayer is for old people, perfect people, boring people, women, and pastors. I want to replace that falsehood with the truth that prayer is 4 everybody.

Prayer is a request for help or an expression of thanksgiving and honor to God. It's like having the most intimate conversation with your best friend you know will not tell your secrets. Only two requirements are necessary:

1. You are willing to talk to God
2. You have the faith that He hears and will answer you.

No special languages, no secret passwords or any particular volumes must be adhered to for God to hear your prayer. He is completely in love with us without prejudice. He may not love every decision we make, but it doesn't change His unconditional love for all of us. It does not shift His plans to have a relationship with us through prayer conversations.

Can you imagine members of your family not speaking to you because they don't agree with everything you've decided to do with your life? You probably would never have a meaningful relationship with them again. God's plan is for families to show each other unconditional love. He reveals this principle to us throughout the Bible. He doesn't turn a deaf ear to His children based on our imperfections or according to the world's or the church's definition of perfection. Embrace that fact and don't allow anything or anyone to keep you from having prayer conversations with God. He's waiting for you.

Prayer Connects Us to God

Prayer was designed as a vehicle to connect us to God and reveal His great desire for us. He wants to be close to us in a personal way. No middleman is required. Unfortunately, the popularity of prayer groups, prayer calls, prayer lists and intercessory prayer at our local churches has made many of us depend on the prayers of middlemen, rather than our prayers. In my opinion, this trend has produced a culture of co-dependency among believers in a way that God never meant. We have become excessively reliant on others to pray on our behalf.

Too many in the church sit back and reminisce about the good old days when miracles were common and people got delivered in one church service. We memorialize Mother So and So and Bishop Whatchamacallit by telling stories of being in services where limbs grew back before our eyes and tumors dried up. We talk about how we miss those days. But why are these miracles not happening anymore? Has God changed? Has His power weakened? Not at all!

In my opinion, God's power is rarely manifested through miracles in these kinds of services because the entire church has stopped praying. We gave it over to a select few. I have nothing against prayer calls, prayer lists, and so forth. In fact, I have led and received from them. However, they were designed as resources for believers to come together and agree. They were never meant to be places that we take our needs and drop them off like dirty laundry for others to pray over.

Numerous examples exist in Scripture of corporate prayers that break chains. Let's look at one of those examples:

(5) But while Peter was in prison, the church prayed very earnestly for him. (6) The night before Peter was to be placed on trial, he was asleep, fastened with two chains between two soldiers. Others stood guard at the prison gate. (7) Suddenly, there was a bright light in the cell, and an angel of the Lord stood before Peter. The angel struck him on the side to awaken him and said, "Quick! Get up!" And the chains fell off his wrists. (8) Then the angel told him, "Get dressed and put on your sandals." And he did. "Now put on your coat and follow me, the angel ordered. (9) So Peter left the cell, following the angel. But all the time he thought it was a vision. He didn't realize it was actually happening. (10) They passed the first and second guard posts and came to the iron gate leading to the city, and this opened for them all by itself. So they passed through and started walking down the street, and then the angel suddenly left him. (11) Peter finally came to his senses. "It's really true!" he said. "The Lord has sent his angel and saved me from Herod and from what the Jewish leaders had planned to do to me!" (12) When he realized this, he went to the home of Mary, the mother of John Mark, where many were gathered for prayer

(Acts 12:5-12, New Living Translation)

Note carefully - they didn't leave it up to a few believers to pray. Everyone participated: young and old. What was the result? A miracle. Yes, we do see miracles when a few people pray but imagine what we would see if we all did our part, instead of leaving it up to our middlemen. Believe it or not, our pastors have now become middlemen we employ to touch God for us. You may say that is a part of their calling. While that is true, it is a serious error to make them our only lifeline to God. It places incredible weight and unfair expectations on them to pray for everyone in the congregation and every small thing they are facing. We exhaust our pastors, drain their energy and then say, "They've lost their anointing" when they underperform or look less than perfect.

We ask intercessors to pray for us and if we don't see results, we blame and shame them. We label them as having no power or relationship with God. However, a look in the mirror would show us that the blame lies in our lap. If we were as committed to praying for ourselves and other believers as we expect our pastors and prayer warriors to be, we would see heaven and earth move when we pray. We can't continue to expect our personal middlemen to have intimacy with God and not seek to have that kind of closeness for ourselves.

We place our names on every prayer list we see on social media and find peace in knowing that someone is praying for us. The prayer list is a God-send because, in the times when you can't find the words to pray for yourself, you have someone to support you in prayer. But if you continually depend on others to pray for you, it reveals your immaturity and lack of discipline, regardless of the length of time you've been a believer.

I want to provoke you to pray, not only seek it. I want you to support others in prayer faithfully. Intercessors, pastors and prayer lists aren't permanent substitutes to fulfill our need to touch God. They are paracletes. They are called to be helpers, not personal worker bees doing all the hard work while you laze about doing nothing. Rejoice in knowing that people are praying for you, but you will discover greater joy in your own lifestyle of prayer.

The point is that middlemen are necessary. However, we don't need them every time we want to communicate with God. He wants a one-on-one relationship. I don't know any couple that wants a middleman in their relationship. Do you? It's like your husband telling someone else to tell you he "loves you" and then you send the messenger back to say "I love you too." It sounds a bit ridiculous, doesn't it? Yet, that's what we do when we depend on other people as our dominant connection to God.

Nobody else can express what you feel about you and your life, like you can, regardless of how much they love you or how long they've known you. God is reaching out to you for personal communion with Him. He doesn't always want a middleman to reach back on your behalf. Using a middleman to respond to God's request to meet Him is like watching a movie and looking for the star but you realize the stunt double (substitute) will be performing the entire movie. We wouldn't stand for it, but it's what we do to God when He taps us for a prayer rendezvous, and we send an understudy.

God makes it crystal clear throughout His Word how much He wants to develop a relationship with us. He uses that same Word to create a desire in us for daily connection with Him.

You didn't choose me. I chose you. I appointed you to go and produce lasting fruit, so that the Father will give you whatever you ask for, using my name

(John 15:16, New Living Translation).

Don't worry about anything; instead, pray about everything. Tell God what you need, and thank him for all he has done. (7) Then you will experience God's peace, which exceeds anything we can understand. His peace will guard your hearts and minds as you live in Christ Jesus

(Philippians 4:6-7, New Living Translation).

You can be a believer who has no relationship with God, but you will miss out on many of the benefits of His beloved sons and daughters. Prayer is 4 you. Prayer is 4 everybody.

Let's Pray

Father, thank You for the line of communication You've opened to me freely and without restrictions. Teach me to pray and rest in knowing You are waiting to hear from me. Create a new desire in me to include You in my life on a daily basis through prayer conversations. Show me how to get the same if not more enjoyment in a prayer conversation with You than I receive from conversations with my friends. In Jesus' name. Amen.

CHAPTER 2

PERFECT PEOPLE NOT ALLOWED

Perfect - complete and correct in every way, of the best possible type or without fault

(Cambridge Dictionary).

*T*he perfect life that is sometimes showcased on television or in the lives of our neighbors doesn't exist, so trying to be perfect is a destination we will never reach. Deciding to wait to be good enough to talk to God will leave us living a guilty existence. The guilty heart will have us to believe we are disappointments to God. It will tell us we are not welcome in His presence when the entire time, His love is waiting for us to receive it.

In our everyday lives, many situations try to make us feel less than qualified, but prayer is not one of them. Prayer introduces us to supernatural peace. We live in it. It's the kind of peace that has no explanation and can only be produced by walking with God.

We live in a social media-driven world, full of photo-shopped pictures that erase every blemish, crooked facial feature or weight-challenged area of our bodies. These images flood our minds long after we see them and are reminders that we are to feel inferior no matter how wonderful we are. Plastic surgery television shows are all the rage. Our eyes and ears are constantly inundated with phrases like "Your nose is too wide." "Your breasts are too small." "You need a bigger butt or bigger muscles." "Your skin is too dark; lighten it." "Your skin is to light; get a tan." All of these things subliminally suggest to us that we aren't okay as we are. They place a bar of perfection in front of us and as we get close to that standard of perfection, the bar is raised and the standards change. Consequently, those of us who buy into the lies are caught up in the futile exercise of trying to be who we are not.

To be clear, I have no problem with plastic surgery or anything that is used to enhance what you look like or who you are. The problem that I have is when we chose to do these things because we feel like we aren't wanted or valued. We engage in these charades because we are not perfect according to the guidelines set, in many cases, by people who don't meet the very guidelines.

We've been given easy access to filters on our phones and social media, so we can always look our best. If by chance we don't use them or use the wrong ones, the internet critics are there. These are people who have been so deeply driven into the slavery of low self-esteem, they try to enslave others by shaming them for posting such an "imperfect" picture. Whether we believe it or not, this feeds the monster of insecurity that tries to overtake our lives.

We read victorious testimonies but are rarely privileged to hear the details that lead to the testimonies, which leave us, in some cases, believing that other people haven't had it as bad as we have. This is common in the church and the secular arena but not with God. Prayer is not a place of competition. There is no rivalry for positions. Prayer is an equalizer. Every believer can pray and expect to receive an answer from God. You don't have to come from the best pedigree or have a diploma, degree or Ph. D. in religious studies. All you need is the desire. All you need is a new appetite for a deeper relationship with our Father.

Guilt encourages us to place ourselves in solitary confinement; a place God never sentenced us to. Guilt is an enemy that will give us erroneous advice, which leads us to run from power, favor, and peace that automatically belongs to us as believers. It comes to steal our peace of mind and pollute the purity of what God wants to build with us. The delusions of perfection that lead us into living guilty lives come to scam and trick us into not collecting the rewards of being believers. Whether it's the look of perfection, educational perfection, spiritual perfection, perfection in our relationships or in our careers, perfection always tries to convince us that we are not yet good enough.

Perfection is an imaginary place that we will never reach, so when we don't see perfection in our lives, it leaves us rehearsing the sad words: "if only." If only I could do it better, it would be perfect. If only I looked like them, I would be perfect. Just say "NO" to perfection and open the door to excellence. Excellence and perfection are two different things. Excellence looks at a situation and says, "I am great; this is great, but how can we make this better." Perfection says, "If everything is not effortless, you've completely failed." The spirit of excellence rewards us, but the burden to be perfect always takes from us. The good news is Jesus wants you before you change one thing. Trust that He is not looking for a way to discredit you or prove how unworthy you are.

Trust is the foundation of a mutually beneficial relationship. In any relationship, whether it is friendly or romantic, if you always feel the other person doesn't trust you or you are always trying to prove you are worthy of that person's time and attention, pretty soon you will stop trying to gain approval. Jesus' blood is the proof that God thought we were worth more than money and are valued far beyond anything natural. He loved us before we became believers and no earthly imperfections can diminish His unfathomable love for us.

His love has been demonstrated time and time again. If you look at every not-so-smart decision you've made in your life, you will find one thing that was always there - God and His love. They have been waiting like the father in the parable of the prodigal son.

(11) To illustrate the point further, Jesus told them this story: "A man had two sons. (12) The younger son told his father, 'I want my share of your estate now before you die. 'So his father agreed to divide his wealth between his sons. (13) "A few days later this younger son packed all his belongings and moved to a distant land, and there he wasted all his money in wild living. (14) About the time his money ran out, a great famine swept over the land, and he began to starve. (15) He persuaded a local farmer to hire him, and the man sent him into his fields to feed the pigs. (16)

Trina McWhorter

The young man became so hungry that even the pods he was feeding the pigs looked good to him. But no one gave him anything. (17) "When he finally came to his senses, he said to himself, 'At home even the hired servants have food enough to spare, and here I am dying of hunger! (18) I will go home to my father and say "Father, I have sinned against both heaven and you, (19) and I am no longer worthy of being called your son. Please take me on as a hired servant." (20) "So he returned home to his father. And while he was still a long way off, his father saw him coming. Filled with love and compassion, he ran to his son, embraced him, and kissed him. (21) His son said to him, 'Father, I have sinned against both heaven and you, and I am no longer worthy of being called your son.'(22) But his father said to the servants, 'Quick! Bring the finest robe in the house and put it on him. Get a ring for his finger and sandals for his feet. (23) And kill the calf we have been fattening. We must celebrate with a feast, (24) for this son of mine was dead and has now returned to life. He was lost, but now he is found. 'So the party begin. (25) "Meanwhile, the older son was in the fields working. When he returned home, he heard music and dancing in the house, (26) and he asked one of the servants what was going on. (27) 'Your brother is back, 'he was told,' and your father has killed the fattened calf. We are celebrating because of his safe return.' (28) "The older brother was angry and wouldn't go in. His father came out and begged him, (29) but he replied, 'All these years I've slaved for you and

14

never once refused to do a single thing you told me to. And in all that time you never gave me even one young goat for a feast with my friends. (30) Yet when this son of yours comes back after squandering your money on prostitutes, you celebrate by killing the fattened calf!' (31) "His father said to him, 'Look, dear son, you have always stayed by me, and everything I have is yours. (32) We had to celebrate this happy day. For your brother was dead and has come back to life! He was lost, but now he is found

(Luke 15:11-32, New Living Translation).

In this parable, we are given the exact illustration of how God feels about us. No matter what ugliness you've chosen to involve yourself in, regardless of your blemished reputation that caused other believers to shun you, God is on the lookout for you. He's expecting you to call Him in your time of need to show you what it feels like to be safe in His arms. Like the brother in the parable, well-meaning people will try to show you every reason you don't deserve God's grace and mercy. They will measure your life against theirs and reward themselves the medal of perfection because they see themselves as more valuable. The truth is God does reward faithfulness, but all of His children are valuable. Whether you've stayed close to walking the line (God's will) or you've zigzagged through life, God has need of you.

So, make a decision to defy guilt, the pressure to be perfect, and everything it tries to impart in your life. Do so by reading God's Word and believing all the good things He promises His children belong to you. Choose to engage in prayer conversations, which will allow you to experience joy, acceptance, and forgiveness like you've never known. Prayer is 4 you. Prayer is 4 everybody.

Let's Pray

Father, I release guilt in every way it has blocked me from communing with You. I realize I don't have to be perfect for You to love me, so I receive the love You offer to me freely. I let go of the heaviness that blinds me to all You have to offer me. I desire to live my best life, and I know that prayer will help me. I walk into a life full of more victory and manifestation. I believe it's Your plan to receive and prosper me regardless of what I've done and what others may think. Help me to become committed to this process of getting to know You on a deeper level. I release myself from the pressure that perfection brings and I trade it for the spirit of excellence. In Jesus' name. Amen.

CHAPTER 3

NO SHADE, ALL LOVE

Shade - To show jealousy or disrespect toward a person in a way that undermines their greatness through words, actions or deeds.

Love - An intense feeling of deep affection that promotes an intimate desire to see someone happy, healthy and at his best.

*T*he terms "throwing shade" or "being shady" are very popular these days. If we check our lives, many of us know people who "throw shade" or act in shady ways. We might be the very ones who do so. The shade kings and queens like to rain on other people's parades by belittling their accomplishments and the things they are happy about; they will give a compliment with a thinly veiled insult attached. This kind of person will find a reason (even if it's made up), why your great is not great enough. The internet is filled with memes and pictures with shady captions and all forms of disrespectful behavior whether or not the person who is being shaded is doing something wonderful or something ratchet.

Social Media promotes shadiness and has stirred up the voyeuristic nature in all of us. We are given box seats as people reveal their private lives for all to see. One minute, they are in love and the next minute they are full of hate and in the middle of an internet war, played out in front of the world. Unbeknownst to us, our understanding of relationships is being shaped by the shadiness of people who don't understand unconditional love and relationships. We take sides in the relationships of people we've never met, people we know little or nothing about simply because they are popular. We cheer them on in their jealous rants and scandalous behaviors.

I know you might be wondering, "What does all of that have to do with prayer?" I'm glad you asked. The way we see and experience natural relationships, love, affection, and intimacy will affect the way we approach or experience God in our relationship with Him. The word "love" is mentioned over 300 times in the King James Bible and even more in other translations, John 3:16 (King James) says: " For

God so loved the world, that he gave his only begotten Son, that whosoever believeth in him should not perish, but have everlasting life." According to this scripture, God's love involves giving and sacrifice. It is not about selfishly and consistently being on the receiving end of the relationship. To many, this can be a foreign concept because, in our reality show-filled DVR'S, a picture of selfish love is celebrated. As we ingest this selfish love, we unknowingly accept dysfunctional behaviors and allow them to enter our lives. Then we wonder why things are going wrong with the people we love. We don't understand that we've removed some of the values from our relationships by embracing mindsets and behaviors that cheapen them.

God is not talking about such cheap love when He says, "He loves us." The fact is that any love worth having will cost those involved something. Closely examine your love relationships and make a conscious decision to evict any behavior that is not conducive to what you deserve and what God has planned for you. If you are always the giver and never the receiver, your love relationship is out of order. I can bet it is negatively affecting the way you see yourself and how you receive God's love. If you are always the receiver, you are out of order as well. You are depleting the resources of the one you say you love. Inevitably, that person will become frustrated and resentful. You are draining them to the point where they are empty. Then you wonder why, all of a sudden, your loved one is acting out of character.

It only takes a look at the way God loves us to see if we are pouring out love or receiving it the way God designed. God thinks we are the bee's knees. He thinks we are special and valuable. Such admiration should be duplicated in all of our relationships. We should pay keen attention to how God treats us and mimic His behavior. He is not abusive. Even His chastisement is motivated by love. His love never leaves us feeling abandoned or cut-off. It never makes us think we have to prove our worth to be accepted by Him. God is omnipresent, omnipotent, and omnipresent. He is sovereign over all. Yet, He has neither found a reason to leave us mortals nor is He searching for one.

Be strong and courageous. Do not be afraid or terrified because of them, for the Lord your God goes with you; he will never leave you nor forsake you

(Deuteronomy 31:6, New International Version).

This should enlighten and empower us to stand up against abuse of any kind: verbal, physical, sexual. As we compare God's love to others we should be able to make the distinction between true love and infatuation or downright deceit. Our understanding should embolden us not to accept the other person's dishonor of who we are as love. God made us all special. We have all been equipped to impact the world from all directions. Your quirks and idiosyncrasies are on purpose. They are to be celebrated, not looked upon as defects. Hence, we should not let others devalue us because of our unique characteristics. If we do, it clearly demonstrates we don't love ourselves, and we are unaware of the quality God has placed in each of us.

Have you ever looked at the snowflakes falling? We are like them. At a glance, they all look the same. However, if you do your research, you will realize no two snowflakes are the same. Yet, they are all beautiful. God sees all His children as uniquely and beautifully designed to manifest His glory on the earth in a distinct way. Check your love patterns to see if they reflect what God models, not what pop culture says is correct.

(16) We know how much God loves us, and we have put our trust in his love. (17) And as we live in God, our love grows more perfect. So, we will not be afraid on the day of judgement, but we can face him with confidence because we live like Jesus here in this world. (18) Such love has no fear, because perfect love expels all fear. If we are afraid, it is for fear of punishment, and this shows that we have not fully experienced his perfect love. (19) We love each other because he loved us first

(1 John 4:16-19, New Living Translation).

The preceding scripture explains that as we learn to trust in God's love for us, we will become perfect (mature) in His love. Moreover, that mature love will flow into every other relationship we are involved in. Trusting in God's love for you is not an opportunity for God to punish you every time you do something outside of His will. Instead, it is an opportunity for Him to show us that His love stands with us regardless of what we do. Fear is the enemy of love. It shows we haven't fully received God's Word when He says "He ain't going nowhere." He means it.

Let us intentionally pray and ask God to reveal to us how to receive unconditional love, as well as give it. This is not a quick process. In my opinion, we learn to love more, as we live and experience more of love. Love is something that is felt and learned. It is inclusive of all the senses, not just emotions. The way we feel is the extent of many of our love experiences, so when the way we feel changes, our commitment to the person or object we've bestowed those feelings upon also changes. Why not allow your love experience to go deeper than how you feel? Let it permeate all your senses. It will give you a sense of how God loves us, how we are to love and be loved.

When our feelings are not the only aspects of our love experiences, we will not let go quickly. We will be prompted to fight to prevent anything from separating us from what we've placed our all into. God fights for us through His Word, to keep us connected and engaged with Him, but we must respond in order for His fight to be effective in our lives.

> *(35) Who shall separate us from the love of Christ? Shall tribulation, or distress, or persecution, or famine, or nakedness, or peril, or sword? (37) Nay, in all these things we are more than conquerors through him that loved us. (38) For I am persuaded, that neither death, nor life, nor angels, nor principalities, nor powers, nor things present, nor things to come, (39) Nor height, nor depth, nor any other creature, shall be able to separate us from the love of God, which is in Christ Jesus our Lord*

(Romans 8:35, 37-39, King James Version).

Nothing will ever separate us from God whether it comes from the outside or inside. Separation is what happens when people can't coexist. It happens when one person believes the other person doesn't receive him or her anymore. Separation is the Enemy's answer to love. Hence, buying into his suggestion that separation must take place when we miss the mark is contrary to God's plan. What is God's plan? Close relationships. Period. No divorce!

God's love reminds me of an old Jennifer Holliday song from "Dream Girls." She sings, "I'm staying; I'm staying and you and you and you, you're gonna love me." This song tells the story of love that runs deep. It's intimate. Intimacy with God should be the goal of every believer. It will require openness, honesty, and vulnerability to God. Too often we try to escape this much-needed transparency because so often, we've had front row seats watching others publicly humiliated and embarrassed. Their darkest secrets were put on blast. God doesn't operate like that.

Vulnerability is a journey. It is longer for some than it is for others. We start this journey by reminding ourselves that God's love won't let us go. Believing in His love lets us understand freedom in a new and exciting way. It changes us for the better. Once we experience the fruit of being unashamed of ourselves in the presence of God, it becomes easier to disrobe emotionally in our prayer times. No one knows what you reveal to God in prayer, but everyone will know you have been in His presence. They will see the difference in you and experience the positive effect it has on you. What's done in the dark comes to the light. Your private intimacy will produce public manifestations of God's presence.

God offers us love without shade, and intimacy without the fear He will expose our confessions spoken in times of worship and weakness. Prayer conversations come with a no-betrayal clause. He won't get mad and seek an opportunity to embarrass you, throw you to the wolves or leave you alone. God's love mirrors the greatest love you've ever experienced in a friendship or romantic relationship times infinity.

Just believing you are never alone and there is someone who wants you even after they've experienced the worst of you, should soften your heart to the idea that *His* love is real love.

We've been betrothed to insecurity and fear for much too long. We need a breakup to make room for agape love (the God kind of love). If you've allowed something else to take up residence in your life, there is no room for God.

Aren't you tired of feeling like something is missing? Aren't you tired of the same old God experiences you've had for years? If your answer is "yes" to any of these questions, the solution will be found in shifting your mindset and perception of God and His relationship with His children.

Believe that receiving pure love and acceptance is possible. With them, you can attract purity in your friendships and romantic relationships. Receiving God's love is the most extreme makeover you will ever have. At first, being convinced that He is always on your team and will always choose you is mind-blowing. However, as you continue to repeat this to yourself it will become just like breathing, second nature. Convincing yourself can be like learning a foreign language. In the beginning, it's hard and may seem impossible, but the more you rehearse, the easier it becomes. Before you know it, you are fluent in that language. The same thing happens as you practice God's love, eventually, you become fluent in His love language, and you will speak it without knowing. It becomes contagious to the other parts of who you are.

Love is patient and kind. Love is not jealous or boastful or proud (5) or rude. It does not demand its own way. It is not irritable, and it keeps no record of being wronged. (6) It does not rejoice about injustice but rejoices whenever the truth wins out. (7) Love never gives up, never loses faith, is always hopeful, and endures through every circumstance

(1 Corinthians 13:4, New Living Translation).

Only God can love as described in the above verse and only God can teach us to love like this. You can't run too far that this His love can't reach you. You can't do something so wrong that His love will leave you, and you are never too old to receive the love that's been waiting for you. Receive It! It's already yours. No shade, all love. Prayer is 4 you. *Prayer is 4 everybody.*

Let's Pray

Father, I believe that Your love is free and requires nothing from me but to receive it. I'm open and stand in expectation of how it will change my life and the way I interact with every person in my life. I commit to acknowledging Your love for me regardless of my actions or behavior. I believe I am special because You've called me Yours. I believe that receiving Your love will allow me to accomplish more and walk with greater compassion for others. Give me a better understanding of intimacy without conditions and allow it to positively affect my entire life. In Jesus' name. Amen.

CHAPTER 4

VALUABLE EXCHANGE

Valuable - Something that is worth a lot, either in terms of money or in terms of being useful or loved.

Exchange - An act of giving one thing and receiving another (especially of the same type or value) in return.

The Oprah Effect

I doubt there are many people on earth who can say they've never heard of Oprah Winfrey. She started her career in journalism in a newsroom, went to a morning show and eventually parlayed that into the "Oprah

Winfrey Show." America had never seen anyone like Oprah. She attracted women of all races and backgrounds. She made you feel as if she really cared about what you had gone through, and she was often prompted to be transparent about her own trials and tribulations, which allowed us to welcome her into our lives. As she grew, she took us along for the trip as new revelation unfolded about her and others. She allowed us to see some of the perks of fame, wealth, and stardom that some of us would never have known existed.

Eventually, she gained the trust of America and the world, so much so, that if Oprah said it, it had to be true. She started a book club and as soon as she released the name of her book for that month, it became a best seller. The author, no matter how obscure he or she was before, became an overnight celebrity. She started a segment of her show called, "Oprah's Favorite Things." She would give the audience her favorite things, and immediately, they would sell out of the items online and in the stores. Oprah built such a reputation that whatever she said was important whether it was about an individual, product or industry. She understood the value of her words, so she spoke about the things that were good to her, and it became profitable for her. I believe this is a perfect example of how God sees the value of our words.

Our words hold just as much weight and have just as much value as Oprah's. The Carolyn Effect. The Sylvester Effect. The Terrence Effect. Whatever your name is, your words have an effect on your life and the world around you. Oprah spoke and in exchange, she was blessed financially. Her status changed. Her vision changed and many other things I'm sure weren't made public. Exchange in prayer is what God desires from us. Though God finds pleasure in meeting us in prayer, it is always more beneficial for us than it is for Him.

"Exchange" in our everyday use of the word means each person gives something of equal value or in some cases one person gives something of lesser value. When it comes to our relationship with God, He always gets the shorter end of the stick, and He accepts it gladly. He is not trying to fill His need because He doesn't have any. However, He does have desires. One of His top desires is for us to realize the depth of His love. Such revelation can only develop through prayer. Prayer makes it hard to resist God's love and the invitation to move into consistent connection with Him. The more we stand in the place of prayer, the more revelation we will recognize. The more we stand in the place of prayer, the more it becomes a part of us. It will become our first stop rather than our last resort. God has been trying to get you to see many things, but the clarity you need to see them only comes

Trina McWhorter

through connection. Prayer lifts the covers off
of the things that were hidden from our natural
eyes. It allows us to see what was there the
whole time. Prayer is an eye- opener. Prayer
lifts the fog.

*The Lord is near to all who call on him, to all who
call on him in truth*

(Psalms 145:18, (New International Version).

"All" means everybody. God is close to
everyone who makes the decision to talk to
Him. He makes having a conversation with
Him as simple as talking to one of our friends.
Just talk. Comfort comes as we choose to talk
to Him; that leads us to recognize the power
alive in our words. That's right, God entrusted
you with power. How will you use it?

*Death and life are in the power of the tongue: and
they that love it shall eat the fruit thereof*

(Proverbs 18:21).

Power lies in what we say and who we say
it to. Whether the words we speak are good
or bad, they transform our mindsets and the
things around us. The moment we understand
how much our words are worth, we will stop
engaging in frivolous conversations, gossip,
and mindless rants. It will teach us to speak
deliberately to those around us and concerning

the situations life brings.

Knowing what the Bible says is essential to our lives. It gives us more meaningful words to speak over our lives, families, and to God. Praying the Word of God is always good because it reveals God's will, His promises and what He has already set in order for us. Having faith in our God-given power lets us walk on water in ways we never imagined. We approach God in prayer without apprehension or fear.

(22) Immediately after this, Jesus insisted that his disciples get back into the boat and cross to the other side of the lake, while he sent the people home.(23) After sending them home, he went up into the hills by himself to pray. Night fell while he was there alone. (24) Meanwhile, the disciples were in trouble far away from land, for a strong wind had risen, and they were fighting heavy waves. (25) About three o'clock in the morning Jesus came toward them, walking on the water. (26) When the disciples saw him walking on the water, they were terrified. In their fear, they cried out, "it's a ghost!" (27) But Jesus spoke to them at once. "Don't be afraid," he said "Take courage. I am here!" (28) Then Peter called to him, "Lord, if it's really you, tell me to come to you, walking on the water. (29) "Yes, come," Jesus said. So Peter went over to side of the boat and walked on the water toward Jesus. (30) But when he saw the strong wind and the waves, he was terrified and

began to sink. "Save me, Lord!" he shouted. (31
Jesus immediately reached out and grabbed him.
"You have so little faith," Jesus said. "Why did you
doubt me?

(Matthew 14:22-31).

We look at this scripture and our attention is immediately drawn to the water-walking miracle. But if we look closer, we will see this was an opportunity for the disciples to trust Jesus in a way they had never done before. The situation led Peter to pray, "Lord, if it's really you, tell me to come to you, walking on the water." The Lord answered Peter with directions, which let him personally experience the power one prayer holds. Peter received instructions, directions, courage, and a demonstration of how Jesus will rescue us. His prayer prompted him to step out on the answer that Jesus gave him.

The next time you face a situation or circumstance that doesn't look favorable. I challenge you to follow Peter's cue. Look at your trial as an invitation to be touched by God, to be given information that may not be obvious. Then watch the demonstration of God's power and the transformation that takes place. Your troublesome situation will create a miracle. Peter dared to pray, and so, he experienced what the other disciples didn't have the courage to do. Like Peter - talk and you will walk.

King Jehoshaphat was another example of talking then walking:

(1) After this, the armies of the Moabites, Ammonites, and some of the Meunites declared war on Jehoshaphat. (2) Messengers came and told Jehoshaphat, "A vast army from Edom is marching against you from beyond the Dead Sea. They are already at Hazazon-tamar."(This is another name for En-gedi.) (3) Jehoshaphat was terrified by this news and begged the Lord for guidance. He also ordered everyone in Judah to begin fasting. (4) So people from all the towns of Judah came to Jerusalem to seek the Lord's help. (5) Jehoshaphat stood before the community of Judah and Jerusalem in front of the new courtyard at the Temple of the Lord. (6) He prayed," O Lord, God of our ancestors, you alone are the God who is in heaven. You are ruler of all the kingdoms of the earth. You are powerful and mighty; no one can stand against you! (7) O our God, did you not drive out those who lived in this land when your people Israel arrived? And did you not give this land forever to the descendants of your friend Abraham? (8) Your people settled here and built this Temple to honor your name. (9) They said, 'Whenever we are faced with any calamity such as war, plague, or famine, we can come to stand in your presence before this Temple where your name is honored. We can cry out to you to save us, and you will hear us and rescue us'. (10) "And now see what the armies of

Ammon, Moab, and Mount Seir are doing. You would not let our ancestors invade those nations when Israel left Egypt, so they went around them and did not destroy them. (11) Now see how they reward us! For they have come to throw us out of your land, which you gave us as an inheritance. (12) O our God, won't you stop them? We are powerless against this mighty army that is about to attack us. We do not know what to do, but we are looking to you for help." (13) As all the men of Judah stood before the Lord with their little ones, wives and children, (14) the Spirit of the Lord came upon one of the men standing there. His name was Jahaziel son of Zechariah, son of Benaiah, son of Jeiel, son of Mattaniah, a Levite who was a descendant of Asaph. (15) He said, "Listen, all you people of Judah and Jerusalem! Listen, King Jehoshaphat! This is what the Lord says: Do not be afraid! Don't be discouraged by this mighty army, for the battle is not yours, but God's. (16) Tomorrow, march out against them. You will find them coming up through the ascent of Ziz at the end of the valley that opens into the wilderness of Jeruel. (17) But you will not even need to fight. Take your position; then stand still and watch the Lord's victory. He is with you, O people of Judah and Jerusalem. Do not be afraid or discouraged. Go out against them tomorrow, for the Lord is with you!" (18) Then King Jehoshaphat bowed low with his face to the ground. And all the people of Judah and Jerusalem did the same, worshipping the Lord. (19) Then the Levites from the clans of Kohath and Korah stood to praise the Lord, the God of Israel, with a very loud shout. (20) Early the next morning the army of Judah went out into the wilderness of Tekoa. On the way Jehoshaphat stopped and said, "Listen to me, all you people of Judah and Jerusalem! Believe in the Lord your God, and you will be able to stand firm. Believe in his prophets, and you will succeed." (21) After consulting the people, the king appointed singers to walk ahead of the army, singing to the Lord and praising him for his holy splendor. This is what they sang: "Give thanks to the Lord; his faithful love endures forever!" (22) At the very moment they began to sing and give praise, the Lord caused the armies of Ammon, Moab, and Mount Seir to start fighting among themselves. (23) The armies of Moab and Ammon turned against their allies from Mount Seir and killed every one of them. After they had destroyed the army of Seir, they began attacking each other. (24) So when the army of Judah arrived at the lookout point in the wilderness, all they saw were dead bodies lying on the ground as far as they could see. Not a single one of the enemy had escaped

(2 Chronicles 20:1-24, New Living Translation).

King Jehoshaphat was told that three different armies were about to attack Judah. He was afraid because he knew they would be destroyed. He realized that only God could get them out, so he called the people together and they began to pray. God gave one of the men in the congregation a prophetic word, which directed them to go to the battle. They won't have to fight, but their enemies would be defeated.

Talking and walking. They prayed (talked to God), got direction and then walked out those directions. So many times we walk then talk. We jump into situations and get into trouble then beg God to get us out. But how much easier would our lives be if we consulted God, first? We blame the Enemy for many of our dilemmas, but the truth is he can only put his hands on certain areas of our lives. Usually, he does so when we jump into places where we have no business being.

I admonish you to seek advice from the best counselor ever - Jesus. One prayer can save you lots of headaches and heartaches. If you start with prayer, you will end in victory. Victory is inevitable with instructions from the One who sees yesterday, today, and tomorrow all at the same time. Victory is yours regardless of the obstacles or the enemies you may face. Prayer helps you build a firm foundation even on shaky ground.

Growing up, we read the story of the three little pigs. They all built houses. One built his house out of straw, and it was destroyed by his adversary. The other built his house out of sticks, and it was destroyed by the same adversary. The third pig had more wisdom and built his house out of brick, so when the enemy came to destroy him and his house, the foundation was too strong to be moved. The third pig realized that it was not smart just to build a house. He figured out the foundation had to be strong because his life depended on it. Tomorrow may bring unexpected situations.

Prayer gives us the wisdom to build a strong foundation so regardless of what we have to face it stays intact. If life's problems threaten portions of your life, you can be confident that your foundation is secure because it was built on prayer. Life's trials and turmoil will not blow you away. Prayer makes the difference in everything you do and all that happens in your life. It is the brick, mortar, and nails that keep you together when everything is falling apart.

Connection - A growing body of research shows that the need to connect socially with others is as basic as the need for food, water and shelter (Matthew Lieberman).

A great amount of research shows that connection through talking and interaction with others is essential to our well-being. Studies show that around twenty-three weeks, babies can hear the daily soundtrack of the mother's heartbeat, the growling of her hungry tummy and will start to hear sounds from the outside world. Hearing their parents' voices while still in the womb helps babies feel attached to them quickly once they are born. In other words, bonding through words starts long before the child and parent ever experience physical touch or before the parents can ever demonstrate to the children that they are loved.

Just as it is with the natural connection, the process to bond with God starts long before we are aware of what is happening to us. God leaves us hints throughout our lives to let us know there is something beyond where we are right now and there is more at work than fate. For example, have you ever been in the middle of doing something or having a conversation and you think, "I've been here before" or "I've seen or heard myself having this conversation"? We call it *déjà vu* but in many circles, it is believed to be a sign that you're in the middle of a God-moment; it's an indicator that you're right where you need to be. When we have these experiences it is up to us to be present in those moments to see what God has planted for us in those places.

These are times of communication not initiated by prayer, but they should provoke us to ask God, "What are you trying to get us to see, experience, understand or gather?" Moments like these should make us slow down to recognize God's hand and His will in that space of time. God-moments make us aware that God is not only there with us, He's also available.

There are moments in time both spiritually and naturally that are more special than others. Birthdays, anniversaries, graduations, and things of that nature are set times we plan to do things we won't normally do. We spend money we would normally save and wear clothes that are not part of our everyday attire. We do all of this to make these moments more memorable.

Just as we set special times, so does God. Several instances in Scripture show there was an appointed time for miracles and shifts to take place. They were not always announced with great fanfare, but they were full of meaning and impartation.

In John 5:1-15, there is a story of a sick man who sat at the pool of Bethesda for thirty-eight years. Every year, an angel would come to stir the water and the first person to enter the water would be healed. This yearly visitation was different from any other. The only thing the people sitting by this pool had to do was recognize this special time of healing and get into the pool. It's the same way with us. As believers, we can't walk around oblivious to the times and seasons. We can't be ignorant of the hints God leaves signaling that this day is different from yesterday. Don't miraculously expect every God-moment to be on our supernatural calendars.

God-moments don't just happen on Sundays. They happen every day and unfold all around us. Prayer makes us sensitive enough to see, hear, and feel God's presence in places that have no crosses or Bibles. The sensitivity that prayer gives us will tell us to move when others are still. It will tell us to say "yes" to opportunities that look lackluster to others but hold spoils for us.

As we seek a better understanding of God and the greater role He desires to play in every aspect of our lives, we will slow down and pay closer attention to our surroundings. God speaks to us through various things, but many times, we miss what He is saying because we are looking for "red seas" to part or bread to start raining down from heaven. I believe these wonder miracles still happen, but at times, God will just whisper. He whispers to sharpen us. mature us, and broaden our views of how He moves and speaks to us.

In 1 Kings 19:11-13(New Living Translation) Elijah experiences a God-whisper. Elijah is running scared because he did what God told him to do and the people didn't like it. They sought to kill him. He hasn't asked God anything; he is just running. He ends up in a cave and God begins to speak to him in an unusual way.

*Go out and stand before me on the mountain,"
the Lord told him. And as Elijah stood there, the
Lord passed by, and a mighty windstorm hit the
mountain. It was such a terrible blast that the
rocks were torn loose, but the Lord was not in the
wind. After the wind there was as earthquake,
but the Lord was not in the earthquake. (12) And
after the earthquake there was a fire, but the
Lord was not in the fire. And after the fire there
was the sound of a gentle whisper. (13) When
Elijah heard it, he wrapped his face in his cloak
and went out and stood at the entrance of the
cave. And a voice said, "What are you doing here,
Elijah?" You would think with the devastation
of the wind, earthquake and fire God would have
something to say, but he didn't. So many times we
are in an uproar about what's going on in our lives,
businesses, families, and in the world and so busy
trying to find God in the midst of the noise, when
he is waiting for us to stop being so captivated
by all of the calamity and quiet ourselves so that
we can hear him. There are times that you won't
hear God, he won't speak, until after the dust has
settled and the parade has ended*

(1 Kings 19:11-13).

A whisper is not heard by everyone; that's
the way it's meant to be. Whispers are only
heard by those in close proximity to the
whisperer. The process of getting in position
for information, instruction, and direction
that others aren't privy to does not only come

from talking to God. It comes from seeking His will and His plan above what we desire. This shifting process is initiated as we first change the posture of our minds when it comes to what we see and experience. Many times we assume that challenging situations we don't like can't possibly be God's will. And so, we never take the time to ask Him. We make logical decisions and don't stop to hear God's perspective on the matter. We permit anxiety to drive us outside of God's plans for us.

God isn't speaking in your storm because He wants you to wait for the whisper. Trouble isn't as intimidating when you believe God has a plan for you. Whether it comes before, during or after the storm - it will be on time. Hearing God-whispers requires a different posture in our hearts, minds, and sometimes our physical stance to declutter us. How we see God and the world will change us and produce a different kind of maturity in our relationship with Him. It will also transform our approach to seeking Him as we detach ourselves from yesterday's junk. We mature from being spoiled children who demand our milk bottles, to people who can handle solid food and become more useful to the kingdom of God. Such growth comes about because we not only pray for ourselves and what we want to see but God can depend on us to pray for others. He can rely on us to pray His will concerning matters that we may see differently from Him.

The privilege of prayer is free, but posture takes sacrifice. Being postured close to God is not always pleasant because posturing requires that you give up your heart's treasures and change your plans to follow God's.

God doesn't always whisper to us directly. Sometimes, He uses people to provide information for our benefit and that of those around us. God releases new ideas in whispers. If we are not mindful of such God-moments, we will miss what we needed because we've taken the person He chose to use for granted.

At times, God purposely doesn't move or speak when we cry out to Him. Rather, He sits with us until after we have labored in prayer and then He shows up. Expect God to whisper in unexpected places and through the least likely people. Ask Him to open your heart to Him so it transcends your time in prayer or is not predicated on whether you are in a spiritual setting or not.

Do you realize we spend more time living our lives than praying about living our lives and doing God's plan? So, if we can't open to Him outside of the intimate space of prayer, we do ourselves and the world a great disservice. God only screams a thing to us after He has whispered to us repeatedly through various things and people. He screams when He finds we are deaf to alternative lines of communication. As we open up for God to whisper through everything and everyone, fresh revelation and new understanding shows up in our lives.

Have you watched a movie or a television show and the scenario mirrored what you were going through? Was something that they mentioned in the movie or episode an answer to what you were asking God? That was a God-moment. God steps into the course of our lives in many unexpected ways. The question is, "Are you open to receiving Him?" So often we hear people say, "Don't put God in a box," and we vow that we never will. We repeat this same mantra to other believers. However, if many of us honestly examine our relationship with Him, we would admit we have done the very thing we said we wouldn't do. We have boxed Him in. In many of our homes and churches, there is a box in the corner labeled, "God."

We open the box only to let Him move within the parameters of our comfort zone, even though discomfort is the bedrock of growth, maturity and new revelation in every area of our lives. We are okay with being discomforted for success in the marketplace, but we'll pump the brakes when we feel the slightest unease in spiritual matters. You can't live this life without discomfort. In my opinion, it is by design. I believe God made it that way to get us to develop on schedule, in every area.

VALUABLE EXCHANGE

When children transition from childhood to adolescence, their voices change; the shape of their bodies changes; what they like to do changes and their attitudes most definitely change. As a result, they are uncomfortable because they are fighting to remain and do things the same, but they are being drawn into a newness that is necessary for them to develop on schedule. Discomfort is a part of natural growth, as well as spiritual growth, but so often, we choose to stunt our growth spiritually, while welcoming our natural growth. If you've found yourself in this place of being too small for the spiritual shoes God wants you to fill, right where you are, give Him the permission to breathe something fresh into your experiences with Him. Allow yourself to develop into everything He wants and needs you to be. I promise, you will be surprised by the things that He has been trying to reveal to you about you.

Our God-boxes bring delay to what God has scheduled for us and then we tend to blame others when we are the ones blocking our progress. Much of the delay is not the Enemy or haters; the delay is your box. Nine times out of ten, God is not the only one in a box, so is your life and destiny. Allowing God to shift your plans will get more to you and let more of His will t flow through you.

47

God Interruptions

Esther is a perfect example of God's plans interrupting our plans. She was favored among all the women in the kingdom to become the new queen. She settled into her new position and everything was well with her - until her uncle sent a message saying that a decree had gone out that all of the Jews be killed. The king was not aware that his new queen was a Jew and signed a law stating all Jews be killed. We pick up the story in Esther 4:1-17, 5:1-3, where her uncle Mordecai is admonishing Queen Esther to be an intercessor with the king for her people, the Jews.

Well, this was no small undertaking even though she was the queen. She had to be invited to come into the king's presence, but if she showed up and he refused to see her, she could be killed. Esther wanted to stay unbothered living in the lap of luxury in the palace but her uncle Mordecai reminded her that judgment would not skip her just because she was married to the king. Esther consented to talk to the king for her people but not before she asked all the Jews to fast and pray for her for three days. Esther's position close to the king was not just so she could be the "baddest" girl in the land. She was chosen on purpose for this particular time in history, as a blessing to her, the king and as an intercessor for her people. The timing was immaculate; it was not a coincidence. The law being signed was not happenstance, but God's plan to set the Jews free. Esther was a conduit of change.

Being close to God comes with bigger perks and responsibilities. Wherever you are positioned on your job, neighborhood or in the body of Christ, you were not placed there just to be blessed. You are there to be a door of promotion for someone else, a hand of favor or light in a dark place. The church has frowned upon people being hungry for positions. However, this can be a good and bad stance to take on this matter. The only reason we should be ashamed of being hungry for a position is if we don't have the grace to fill it and bring something to the office. Proper positioning is necessary to institute change in places outside of the church. The president of a company can change the lives of more people than the person in the mailroom. There is nothing wrong with being in the mailroom, but it limits what is accessible to you. It limits your ability to make impactful decisions that can improve the lives of those around you. It limits who listens to you and how they respond to the information you have. Your information may be correct but the respect is different because of your position. God will give us the desire for elevation and promotion, spiritually and naturally, to position us for power moves. The greater the positioning the greater the grace you will need to be successful in it. Do you have the power (grace) for the moves you want to make? If not, the power can be released to you as you pray and seek the will of the Father.

Let's Pray

Father, we bless You for showing us how valuable we are. We are open to speaking to You because we are sure You are waiting for our words. We want to draw closer to You. We want to be blessed and be blessings to others. So teach us how to transition from being babes into being knowledgeable, seasoned believers. We give You permission to step into the course of our lives and uncover more of who we are and what You've purposed us to do. Meet us in unexpected places, so we may expand our views of who You are and how You desire to interact with us. In Jesus' name. Amen.

CHAPTER 5

FAITH

"Faith is taking the first step even when you don't see the whole staircase"

(Dr. Martin Luther King Jr.).

*H*ebrews Chapter 11 is full of examples of faith. It starts by explaining to us that walking by faith produces a good reputation. That is to say, when people gave descriptions of those depicted throughout this chapter, faith was always included. The saints in the scriptures were always concerned about legacy. Included in their legacies was the honor of their names. Such honor dictated how their families would be received after they passed away. Many years ago, there was a popular song that said: "Only what you do for Christ will last." This rings true to this very day.

If we reflect on our interactions with other believers, the people who left the greatest impact on our lives were those we saw walking in faith. Seeing that their faith produced what they believed and more influenced us. We like to tell the stories of the mothers in the church who prayed for drunken men in our services. The stories go that when these women were finished praying, the drunk men were sober. Or when someone had a loved one in prison, the saints prayed and the person was released.

These days, we don't see as much of that kind of faith that produces what looks impossible, because we are blessed with the extras in life. We are so full, we've forgotten that emptiness is still possible. FYI ⬚ lack of money is not the only way to be empty. Many of us don't lack finances, but our health is poor. The doctor's prognosis is not good. Praying in faith is the only way to change this kind of situation. Faith transforms and opens the door for miracles, signs, and wonders in our lives. Regardless of how much you pray or how eloquent your words are, if faith is not the largest component of your prayer, you will not get the results you are expecting.

God promised Sara she would conceive a child even though she and her husband Abraham had gotten too old according to the laws of nature. However, they believed in the faithfulness of God, and Sara's body was restored to not only conceive a child but to deliver it.

Faith empowers your prayers to produce what the Word says they should. The power in prayer comes through perseverance and perseverance builds muscle. When you set a goal to build your muscles, it doesn't happen the first time you go to the gym. In fact, the first few times you go, the pain makes you want to quit. Nonetheless, as you stay focused on your goal and have faith in your ability to accomplish it, you start to see results. You resist the temptation to settle for less. The weight you've placed on those muscles produces the six-pack you want.

The same determination we have in the gym should carry over into our prayer lives. Push yourself in prayer to build your spiritual muscle, so that doubt no longer has a place in your prayers. Push yourself to have a six-pack in the things of God. It's important that we have some kind of muscle in our faith before we need to use it. That makes sense because trying to build your faith in the midst of a situation is one of the hardest things to do. When life is going well, it tends to lull us into thinking it will stay that way forever. However, from my own experience and watching others, no one is always on the mountaintop. Sooner or later, we have some valley situations that we must face. Faith is the best outfit you can wear in those valley places.

Money can't buy faith. Faith is free, but it costs. The only currency you can use is forgetfulness. Forgetting what the world says is impossible. Forgetting that you're not supposed to defy natural laws by just believing that God will supernaturally change things.

Making the decision to build your faith is free, but the process to build it is expensive. I spoke about this in a previous chapter, but it is worth repeating. Spending time studying the Bible is the expense that comes with building your faith. Consistently talking to God is another expense. The most expensive element, however, is walking out what you've learned in prayer and in the Word of God.

24) Jesus went with him, and all the people followed, crowding around him. (25) A woman in the crowd had suffered for twelve years with constant bleeding. (26) She had suffered a great deal from many doctors, and over the years she had spent everything she had to pay them, but she had gotten no better. In fact, she had gotten worse. (27) She had heard about Jesus, so she came up behind him through the crowd and touched his robe. (28) For she thought to herself, "If I can just touch his robe, I will be healed." (29) Immediately the bleeding stopped, and she could feel in her body that she had been healed of her terrible condition. (30) Jesus realized at once that healing power had gone out from him, so he turned around in the crowd and asked, "Who touched my robe?" (31) His disciples said to him, "look at this crowd pressing around you. How can you ask, 'Who touched me?" (32) But he kept on looking around to see who had done it. (33) Then the frightened woman, trembling at the realization of what had happened to her, came and fell to her knees in front of him and told him what she had done. (34) And he said to her, "Daughter, your faith has made you well. Go in peace. Your suffering is over

(Mark 5:24-34, New Living Translation).

Everything about this set up should have discouraged this woman from even trying to touch Jesus. A crowd of people was around Him; all of them trying to touch Him to see what He was going to do. He was already on the way to heal somebody else and last, but not least, according to Levitical law, she wasn't supposed to be around people until she stopped bleeding. This woman's faith caused her to go against the laws, to press past everyone else because she believed that her healing, her change, was in touching Jesus' robe. Her faith opened up the path that led her right to the feet of Jesus and - it produced. Had she continued to look at the crowd trying to figure out how she was going to get to His robe, she would have missed her opportunity to change everything about her life.

See, our focus is mainly on the healing of her body, but that was not the only factor in this miracle. Moving in faith allowed her to have relationships again because she couldn't be around anyone while she was bleeding. This situation had gone on for twelve years, so it had been over a decade since someone gave her a simple hug or held her hand. Faith brought her from being broke back to a place of financial security. As we read in the story, she spent all of her money in the doctor's office and she got worse instead of getting better. So, this one leap of faith cemented her place in the scriptures and changed her entire life.

The overflow from her healing was not just for her; it was also a testimony to the crowd. Jesus stopped the crowd and asked, "Who touched me?" and after He asked a few times, she came forth. This was a witness to someone in that crowd who needed an example of what faith could do and the power of God. That person saw that her faith made the difference in her touch. Many people touched Jesus but no virtue left Him. Faith made the difference.

Faith is the key that puts you in the place to touch God. Just like the woman with the issue of blood, your faith will produce the thing you are asking for. It will flood the other areas of your life. God will deliberately position us in places that make us uncomfortable. Uncomfortable places are often our set locations for miracles and change. They are places for God to be glorified and for us to be living testimonies in the eyes of those He has strategically positioned around us. Every person God plants around you is not a friend. The same people who watched the woman suffer and shunned her for twelve years were the same people who had front-row seats at her comeback. It is necessary for the enemies who watch us suffer, to watch us recover.

You prepare a feast for me in the presence of my enemies. You honor me by anointing my head with oil. My cup overflows with blessings

(Psalm 23:5, New Living Translation).

Faith will keep you focused on God and not on whether your surroundings look favorable.

Faith Is the Foundation

Through faith we understand that the worlds were framed by the word of God, so that things which are seen were not made of things which do appear

(Hebrews 11:3, King James Version).

God used faith in the recipe to frame the world. So, if it was in the foundation of what our Father was creating, it should definitely be in the foundation of whatever we endeavor to put together in our churches, for our families, our businesses and anything we desire God to prosper. If we really put this scripture in perspective, we will notice everything is faith. The ground we stand on is faith. The air we breathe is faith. The ocean and the seafood in it are faith. The sun, moon, and stars are faith. It's hard to deny the need for something that we participate in every day. It's not exactly wise to refuse to use what God believed He needed in creation. How much better would your life be if you used everything that God offers? You win before the battle when you seek God first in prayer. Prayer is 4 you. Prayer is 4 everybody.

Let's Pray

Father, I pray that You were glorified and Your people will be edified by what you've given me to share. I pray that faith is restored and ignited in those who dare to believe there is more to know about You. Allow Your people to see exponential growth from their perseverance in prayer. Allow this journey to be full of joy and peace that surpasses their understanding and a new rest that they've never known. Demonstrate the perks of prayer in everything they touch. Sustain them in times of pain, disappointment and in every valley they may face. Allow the things they've learned or agreed with to be so life-changing they positively affect everyone around them. In Jesus' name. Amen.

MEDITATION SCRIPTURES

But without faith it is impossible to please him: for he that cometh to God must believe that he is, and that he is a rewarder of them that diligently seek him

(Hebrews 11:6, KJV).

But seek ye first the kingdom of God, and his righteousness; and all these things shall be added unto you

(Matthew 6:33, KJV).

For as the body without the spirit is dead, so faith without works is dead also

(James 2:26, KJV).

And this is the confidence that we have in him, that, if we ask any thing according to his will, he hearth us: (15) And if we know that he hear us, whatsoever we ask, we know that we have the petitions that we desired of him

(1 John 5:14-15, KJV).

Pray without ceasing

(1 Thessalonians 5:17, KJV).

You don't have enough faith," Jesus told them. "I tell you the truth, if you had faith even as small as a mustard seed, you could say to this mountain, "Move from here to there,' and it would move. Nothing would be impossible

(Matthew 17:20, NLT).

For we walk by faith, not by sight

(2 Corinthians 5:7, KJV).

So then faith cometh by hearing, and hearing by the word of God

(Romans 10:17, KJV).

Thou wilt keep him in perfect peace, whose mind is stayed on thee: because he trusteth in thee

(Isaiah 26:3, KJV).

I pray that God, the source of hope, will fill you completely with joy and peace because you trust in him. Then you will overflow with confident hope through the power of the Holy Spirit

(Romans 15:13, NLT).

(13) You made all the delicate, inner parts of my body and knit me together in my mother's womb. (14) Thank you for making me so wonderfully complex! Your workmanship is marvelous-how well I know it. (15) You watched me as I was being formed in utter seclusion, as I was woven together in the dark of the womb. (16) You saw me before I was born. Every day of my life was recorded in your book. Every moment was laid out before a single day had passed. (17) How precious are your thoughts about me, O God. They cannot be numbered! (18) I can't even count them; they outnumbered the grains of sand! And when I wake up, you are still with me

(Psalms 139:13-18, New Living Translation).

Trust in the Lord with all your heart; do not depend on your own understanding. (6) Seek his will in all you do, and he will show you which path to take. (7) Don't be impressed with your own wisdom

(Proverbs 3:5-7, New Living Translation).

(1) The Lord is my light and my salvation-so why should I be afraid? The Lord is my fortress, protecting me from danger, so why should I tremble? (2) When evil people come to devour me, when my enemies and foes attack me, they will stumble and fall. (3) Though a mighty army surrounds me, my heart will not be afraid. Even

if I am attacked, I will remain confident. (4) The one thing I ask of the Lord- the thing I seek most- is to live in the house of the Lord all the days of my life, delighting in the Lord's perfections and meditating in his temple. (5) For he will conceal me there when troubles come; he will hide me in his sanctuary. He will place me out of reach on a high rock. (6) Then I will hold my head high above my enemies who surround me. At this sanctuary I will offer sacrifices with shouts of joy, singing and praising the Lord with music. (7) Hear me as I pray, O Lord. Be merciful and answer me! (8) My heart has heard you say, "Come and talk with me." (9) Do not turn your back on me. Do not reject your servant in anger. You have always been my helper. Don't leave me now; don't abandon me, O God of my salvation! (10) Even if my father and mother abandon me, the Lord will hold me close. (11) Teach me how to live, O Lord lead me along the right path, for my enemies are waiting for me. (12) Do not let me fall into their hands. For they accuse me of things I've never done; with every breath they threaten me with violence. (13) Yet I am confident I will see the Lord's goodness while I am here in the land of the living. (14) Wait patiently for the Lord. Be brave and courageous. Yes, wait patiently for the Lord

(Psalm 27, New Living Translation).

My Prayer for You

Father, I'm grateful that You have allowed Your sons and daughters to read and glean from what You have given me. I pray that they would feel the tug of prayer as they go through their day. I pray that they would respond eagerly to Your wooing to join You in prayer rendezvous. Allow their connections and conversations with You to become a place of comfort and peace. Give them the desire to start prayer conversations with You and remain disciplined through the ups and downs of life. Open their ears to hear as You speak to them. Open their eyes to see the answers to their prayers that You place in their path. Remove doubt that would keep them from responding to Your call.

Father, bless them with the desires of their hearts and allow them to know You in ways that aren't common. Stir up hunger and thirst for You that will cause them to run to You first. Demonstrate Your power in their lives and reward their new commitment to prayer. In Jesus' name. Amen.

36930690R00043

Made in the USA
Columbia, SC
27 November 2018